SALES
SECRETS
TODAY

SALES
SECRETS
TODAY

How to BECOME a

SALES PROFESSIONAL

&

INCREASE SALES

REVISED AND UPDATED 2020

Mark W. Shaughnessy

ARPress
ILLUMINATING IDEAS.
EMPOWERING VOICES

ARPress
45 Dan Road Suite 5
Canton MA 02021
Hotline: 1(888) 821-0229
Fax: 1(508) 545-7580

Ordering Information:
Quantity sales. Special discounts are available on quantity purchases by corporations, associations, and others. For details, contact the publisher at the address above.

Printed in the United States of America.

ISBN-13:   Softcover   979- 8-89330-214-1
                     eBook   979- 8-89330-213-4
Library of Congress Control Number: 2024901017

Sales Professional

Sales Secrets Today includes time-proven strategies for salespeople to achieve greater success, higher income, and rapid career advancement.

Sales Secrets Today provides Critical Success Factors to elevate a salesperson's performance and enhance their ability to succeed in today's competitive marketplace.

Learn how to master the "Sales Process" and explore modern sales and marketing techniques for superior results.

Companies benefit from a steady income stream that ensures continued growth and a comfort level in the planning process.

Benefits of *Sales Secrets Today*:
- Improve productivity.
- Provides the company with steady revenue.
- Enjoy more time with family and friends.

Sales Secrets Today is a must read for those who want to increase their income and become a Sales Professional.

DEDICATION

A special dedication to my cousin Bill Shaughnessy, a highly successful salesman for the Prudential and a wonderful person.

DISCLAIMER

Although these secrets have been used successfully by others, there is no guarantee that they will work for everyone. This sales process is relevant for all sales professions even though it does not cover all the products and services being offered in the marketplace.

REVISED AND UPDATED

As the sales process evolved and time became even more precious, revisions were made to enhance the format and readability of this material.

ACKNOWLEDGEMENTS

Thanks to all the great teachers, managers and writers who provided me the guidance, knowledge and inspiration that allowed me to achieve more than I could have on my own.

For those authors where I use material that I read over the years but cannot identify the specific writer, I thank you for allowing me to share your wisdom.

My appreciation goes to those special sales reps who succeeded using the ideas presented in this narrative when others doubted the process.

TABLE OF CONTENTS

ABOUT THE AUTHOR

Mark Shaughnessy is a graduate of Kent State University and has built and revitalized sales and marketing organizations as a sales manager and senior vice president of sales and marketing.

He transformed sales organizations from being ineffective to exceeding goals. When promoted, the sales organizations continued to perform successfully due to his training programs.

Mark represented large companies such as The Prudential Insurance Company, Blue Cross & Blue Shield of Georgia, Jefferson-Pilot and Ceridian; each presenting a different challenge. He also learned valuable lessons while participating in start-up companies.

At Ceridian, sales increased more than 50% in successive years. Mark received the coveted Chairman's Award for sales leadership, not presented in the prior five years.

Sales Secrets Today represents the best ideas for learning the sales profession. These principles provide the process to enable the salesperson to become a Sales Professional and prosper for years.

Mark has also written **Management Rules***, *How to Effectively Manage Any Organization to Success.* Mark and his brother Don coauthored *Vietnam Remembered Today.* *

His latest books are novels that provide a view of the corporate world based on Mark's experiences in business. He reveals what happens inside companies that struggle to stay in business by changing their strategies and what happens when they don't. *Conflicted* and *Attempted Murder* will be published and available by the end of 2023 and available through: mwswriter@gmail.com or by phone: 706-326-1777

*Books available through Amazon.com

INTRODUCTION

"If you believe you can or believe you can't,
in both cases you are probably right."

Henry Ford

Sales Secrets Today was developed with a few simple objectives:

- **Increase Sales**
- **Provide A Proven Sales Process**
- **Quick and Easy to Implement**

Sales Secrets Today is a process to achieve superior results through a strategic approach to the marketplace.

Individuals Benefit:

- ✓ *Increase Income*
- ✓ *Improve Quality of Life*
- ✓ *Enjoy Faster Career Advancement*

Organizations Benefit:

- ➤ **Generate More Revenue**
- ➤ **Experience Greater Growth**
- ➤ **Increase Profits**

Adopt the modern sales model in *Sales Secrets Today* to become a Sales Professional. These concepts will help you increase sales, achieve a higher income, and enjoy a successful career.

SECTION A

SALES SUCCESS

I. SUCCESS HABITS

"You can't leap a chasm in two bounds."
Chinese Proverb

A. OVERVIEW

Successful people pursue new ways in their approach to achieve greater sales results. Just like a chain is only as strong as its weakest link, you must embrace *all* these concepts to become a total Sales Professional.

Prospects and customers want to do business with knowledgeable salespeople, so strive to become an expert in each product or service you offer.

The secret is to continually learn new techniques.

B. MAKE THE COMMITMENT

To reach your goals, commit yourself to becoming the top sales person in your company. Most people don't fully commit to achieving an objective. Rather, they want something, but don't clearly define it.

"You must believe it before you see it," to quote Dr. Wayne Dyer, a noted author of self-development books.

C. LAW OF ATTRACTION

The Law of Attraction states that unexpected circumstances emerge that allow you to achieve your desired objectives. Nobody knows all the details of how a mission will be completed but when you understand the sales process better, unforeseen opportunities will arise that enables you to accomplish your goals.

D. MARKETING MESSAGE/SALES STATEMENT

Develop a succinct marketing message, that is, a brief sales statement or elevator speech to describe what you do to help your customers. This 15-30 second message headlines the value you provide to a client. For example.

"We help companies and individuals increase sales."

"We reduce the cost of health care by reviewing large claims."

"We specialize in turning around small companies."

E. CRITICAL SUCCESS FACTORS (CSF)

Adopt the following Critical Success Factors:

1. **Develop Your Sales Process**

2. **Establish Goals**

3. **Prepare Marketing Strategies**

4. **Increase Prospecting**

5. **Enhance Telephone Techniques**

6. **Implement Time Management Principles**

7. **Master Presentation Skills**

8. **Learn Negotiating Process**

9. **Improve Communication Capabilities**

The secret to become a complete Sales Professional is to embrace ALL Critical Success Factors.

F. DO IT NOW!

Begin to use these techniques today and don't get paralysis through analysis. Put these strategies, ideas and concepts into your daily work and Do It Now!

G. PEAK TO PEAK SALES

Peak to peak selling is to be a consistent producer of sales results while eliminating the peaks and valleys of sales. Make a sale regularly, whether daily, weekly, or monthly, regardless of the size or amount. Eliminate Peak and Valley selling as it is an emotional roller coaster that is discouraging and is to be avoided.

H. QUANTUM LEAP STRATEGY

The Quantum Leap Strategy is designed to make significant improvements in sales with far greater results than previously achieved. The high achiever referred to as the "hunter" or "rainmaker," gains this status through unprecedented sales.

Assess the potential in the market and prepare strategies to achieve superior results. Ask the simple question, "How can I maximize my sales results?"

Discover new ways to approach the market; e.g., focus on larger prospects and customers, sell more expensive items or negotiate higher profit margins.

The secret to make a Quantum Leap is to discover new ways to market your products and services to qualified buyers.

I.   GET OFF TO A GREAT START

Salespeople tend to perform the same throughout their careers as they do during their first year of business. When they start fast, they are successful for years. Those salespeople that have a slow start tend to remain behind their peers.

The most successful learn their products quickly, study the sales process and embrace best practices from other successful salespeople. Develop and discuss strategies with veteran reps and managers to develop the habit of closing sales.

Close a sale to learn the implementation process and how to perform tasks. Make the effort to get a sale to gain the confidence and momentum to excel.

J.   PARETO PRINCIPLE

Based on the Pareto 80/20 Principle, 20% of your prospects and clients yield 80% of your results. Identify the Ideal Customer and learn the process for qualifying prospects and spend your time on the best prospects and clients.

The secret is to focus your efforts on the top 20% of prospects and clients.

K. SUCCESS HABITS

Stick to a routine using Critical Success Factors until they become second nature. Adopt a new technique for twenty-one days and it will become an acquired habit.

L. BE THE BEST

The sales leader sets targets based on the market potential and developed a plan to exceed prior milestones. The superstar achieves goals by developing strategies to accomplish them.

"Not doing more than the average is what keeps the average down."

William Winans

M. CODE OF ETHICS

Follow a strong code of ethics in business:

- **Don't talk negatively about competitors.**
- **Sell only what your company can support.**
- **Meet all commitments to your customers.**

When you deviate from a code of ethics, you compromise the integrity of your company. Always consider what is best for the customer and it will be best for you as well.

N. MASTERMIND PRINCIPLE

Form a 'Mastermind' group with positive like-minded people and meet regularly to share ideas, discuss problems, and create solutions to gain different perspectives on issues.

Meetings produce ideas to improve performance such as product enhancements, sales ideas, marketing concepts, competition, pricing, and customer service issues. Further, these may be discussed with management to represent marketplace needs.

O. BRAINSTORMING

Brainstorming sessions encourage participants to provide ideas and solutions for further consideration. This approach creates a positive atmosphere of inclusion without restrictions. Discuss ideas in detail only after they all have been presented.

The secret to brainstorming is to allow ideas to flow freely and not to judge them as they are presented.

P. KNOW YOUR SALES STYLE

Those who have been told that they would be good in sales often discover they are in the wrong sales position.

The secret is to know that some salespeople are best suited for inside sales and others are outside sales oriented.

Inside salespeople are more comfortable when customers come to them. For example, in retail sales, the store advertising creates the customer demand. "Call reluctance," the fear of calling strangers or clients, prevents some from being successful in outside sales. These same salespeople excel when prospects come to them as their personality delights the customer.

The external salesperson will approach others via the telephone or in person. Outside salespeople are willing and eager to contact new prospects. Either sales role can be successful and when people are in the position for which they are best suited they are more likely to reach their full potential.

Q. PERSONAL DEVELOPMENT

Prepare a plan to ensure you are fully trained in all aspects of the business. If your company does not support these needs, then you must seek them on your own.

Gain knowledge about your company, competitors, and the industry. In addition, focus on sales skills, presentation techniques, negotiating strategies, and communication skills to become the total rep, a Sales Professional.

There are few salespeople with ten years' experience, but many who have one year's experience ten times.

Read Every Day: Successful people read thirty minutes to one hour every day. Read a book each month on sales, sales management, leadership or other related topics and it will have a powerful impact in a short period of time.

"Those who don't read are no better off than those who can't."

Brian Tracy

You'll discover new ways to approach work and how others accomplish their goals. Books on sales and sales management guide you on what should be done and how to do it. Leadership books provide an overall perspective on business and ethics that prepares you for your future.

"Not all readers are leaders, but all leaders are readers."

Reading provides the foundation for more effective communication and improves your personal performance. A better understanding of business enables you to speak more confidently about company and industry strategies. This unique advantage separates you from other sales reps and builds credibility with prospects, customers, and distributors.

Industry journals and business magazines such as the *Wall Street Journal, Forbes, Fortune,* and *Business Week* provide in-depth information on successful companies and individuals.

Seminars: Professional salespeople attend seminars on strategic selling, time management and presentations skills.

R. MODELING

One popular method to achieve the same success as other sales leaders is "modeling" or to copy actions and a style of successful people. Invite the top salespeople to lunch and ask them how to improve your effectiveness. Several ideas identified and corrected could put you on the right track. Sales leaders are not selfish and they will help.

S. MULTI-TASKING IS OVERRATED

When people try to do more than one thing at one time the result is disastrous to you, the person you interact with and the work you try to complete.

The secret to become more effective and efficient is to complete one task at a time.

When on the telephone, don't read your e-mail, or proofread written correspondence. Listen closely to the caller's intentions. Focus on one task, complete it and then move on to the next project.

This chapter is the foundation for the more specific information to follow. Each chapter will focus on a particular part of the sales process that is, in turn, part of building a successful sales plan.

What's more, each aspect along the spectrum of the sales process reinforces the other to form a complete plan that enables the salesperson to understand the sales process and become a Sales Professional.

NOTES

II. GOAL ACHIEVEMENT

"If you don't know where you are going,
any road will take you there."
Kordan

A. GOAL SETTING

The Sales Professional establishes a Personal Sales Plan to accomplish sales goals. The key is to know HOW you will achieve your goals, i.e., specific action steps defined to meet your objectives. Following is the goal setting process.

B. INCOME GOALS

Your desired income establishes your sales goal and the compensation plan allows you to calculate the sales required. A goal to earn $100,000 a year and the company pays ten percent commission on each sale, a sales target of $1,000,000 yields the desired compensation.

The secret to successful salespeople is to define their goals and develop strategies to accomplish them.

A person sets goals each year-end using several factors; the number of new accounts and average revenue per sale.

Identify target markets, locations, and target audiences to approach new prospects and existing clients as well.

Decide on what specific steps you must make to generate the activity required to meet your goals, e.g., number of proposals, presentations, phone calls, mailings, etc. Finally, what do you need to prepare to make your goals a reality, e.g., training in certain aspects of sales, such as improving your close ratio, telephone techniques, letter writing, marketing materials, etc.

C. SMART METHOD TO SET GOALS

The first step to achieve your goals is to meet the SMART test; Specific, Measurable, Achievable, Rewarding and Time based.

S-Specific. Be clear in describing what you want to achieve. For example, "I will reach one million dollars in sales this year in order to make $100,000."

M-Measurable. The goals must be quantifiable. "I will sell fifty units each year." Most sales reps miss their goals either because they go for the big sale or they make a lot of smaller sales that don't add up to their quota.

A-Achievable. Can these goals be achieved and are you committed to them? Are they realistic or are you doomed to fail by setting unrealistic goals?

R-Rewarding. Does the goal motivate you? Can you buy a new home, or car, or achieve an income goal, or receive a promotion when you exceed your goals?

T-Time-based. Goals must have a time frame to complete, e.g., this year, this quarter, month, week, or each day, etc.

Example: "My goal for this year is to sell $1 million of new revenue and make $100,000 in commissions, sell 50 units at an average of $20,000 each in order to buy a home." This goal is specific, measurable, achievable, rewarding, and time-based.

"By failing to prepare, you are preparing to fail."
Benjamin Franklin

D. WRITE DOWN YOUR GOALS

Write down goals and keep them prominently displayed so you will be reminded to accomplish them. Simply thinking that you want to be the sales leader and wanting to make a lot of money is not good enough. Sales leaders set clearly defined goals of being the top producer in the company and they state specifically how much money they expect to earn.

Case Study

A study at Yale several years ago showed that of a graduating class, sixty-eight percent of the students didn't have defined goals, twenty-nine percent had stated their goals, but only three percent wrote out their goals. Thirty years later, the three percent who wrote down their goals accomplished more financially than all of the other students combined. The only difference was their commitment to write down their goals.

E. BREAK DOWN GOALS

A $1 million-dollar goal become more manageable when broken down to annual, quarterly, monthly or weekly goals: Quarterly-$250,000*, Monthly-$84,000*, Weekly-$21,000* *Rounded. Sell four units a month at an average transaction of $21,000, or $84,000 per month.

The secret is to break down your goals into smaller amounts, write down your goals and strategies, and review them daily.

F. ALIGN OBJECTIVES WITH ORGANIZATION

Your goals should align with the rest of the organization to ensure resources are available to support your sales efforts.

If your plan is to sell mostly product A, but you sell more of product B, you may encounter a shortage of supplies and staff to service your new customers. Sell the right mix of products to ensure the company can fulfill customers' expectations.

However, you don't want to pass up sales opportunities, so it is best to discuss extraordinary circumstances with management. You may find that the product you are about to sell is just the boost it needs to make it a viable offer.

Any sale is important and helps the company remain in business and flourish. Positive and frequent communication among the client, salesperson and the departments that service the customer should be ongoing. Remain committed to conquering each step throughout the process and you will achieve your goals.

G. BARRIERS TO SUCCESS

Identify the barriers that prevent you from achieving your goals. Assess your skills in critical areas; time management, prospecting, presentations, negotiating and communication.

Prepare a list of features and benefits, your USP, advantages versus the competition and responses to questions and objections to sell your products and services. Professional salespeople don't wing it; they learn the process of selling and they become Sales Professionals.

- **Are you skilled at time/territory management?**
- **Do you ask for referrals?**
- **Are you comfortable calling others?**
- **Do you have a qualified list of prospects to call?**
- **Can you sell the value of your products?**

Identify how to improve your sales and self-management skills such as reporting, telephone techniques, presentation strategies, communication skills, and other important tasks. List the action steps to be taken to overcome these obstacles.

Barriers	Action Steps
Time Management	Read *The Time Trap*
Telephone Techniques	Go to a sales seminar
Sales Skills	Read *Sales Secrets Today*

Prepare, Plan & Review: When you set your sights on ambitious outcomes, you become more open to new ways to achieve them. Prepare a plan to define goals, strategies and action steps in one document. Review monthly to assess progress and adjust your approach to achieve your goals.

"A goal is a dream with a deadline."
Napoleon Hill

III. SALES PROCESS

"You can close more business in two months
by becoming interested in other people than you can
in two years by trying to get people interested in you."

Dale Carnegie

A. SALES OVERVIEW

The primary purpose of a salesperson is to gain and keep customers. Time is of the essence for both the salesperson and the prospect. Quality salesmanship should be concise yet thorough when talking with prospects and customers.

You and the prospect don't have the time to meet only to find out there is no need or the prospect does not qualify.

The secret to sales is to quickly qualify a prospect, uncover a need and provide a solution to their problem.

The sales process is universal in its approach. That is, there are certain steps taken on a consistent basis that are used to successfully complete sales regardless of the product or service.

Sales Secrets Today includes the steps necessary to achieve your goals and become a Sales Professional. It is vitally important to embrace them all. Note that the approach toward new prospects and existing clients is virtually the same.

Elephant Hunt. Do not rely on one big sale to reach your sales goals. Meet your quota each month through consistent sales. Elephant hunting is the curse of the big game hunter: Feast or famine.

B. KEYS TO HIGHER SALES

1. Increase New Sales

2. Sell Multiple Products Per Sale

3. Sell More Products to Clients

1. INCREASE NEW SALES

The best way to experience long-term growth is to sell a greater number of new accounts. Assess the potential market and develop a marketing plan to reach out to viable prospects. Sales leaders focus their attention on those prospects that provide the greatest opportunity.

Identify key prospects: The first step toward building a sales funnel is to identify your key prospects that meet your qualifications. Lists can be purchased or are available on the Internet that identify prospects by name, industry, profession, number of employees, SIC code, revenue, or by zip code and compare them to your Ideal Customer Profile.

Sales strategies may consist of phone calls, letters, advertising or website campaigns. Establish an approach to each prospect and set deadlines to complete each task.

Prospect	Method	Due Date	Complete
	P-Phone		
	M-Mail		
	A-Advertising		
	W-Website		

2. SELL MORE PRODUCTS PER SALE

Selling multiple products as an up-sell or cross-sell may increase the average sale by twenty-five percent or more. Examples of a cross-sell are to add a dryer along with a washer, upgrade to a better option, add a warranty and much more.

Understand the customers overall needs and add other products or services that benefit the customer and increase the sales volume. Seek out prospects that can use more than one of your products or services.

3. SELL MORE PRODUCTS TO CLIENTS

Typically, the fastest and lowest cost way to increase sales immediately is to evaluate your current customer list to determine who would benefit from other products and services.

Strategies for selling to clients: Sales to a client are cheaper in terms of cost, time and effort. Satisfied customers will meet to discuss other products when you understand their needs and as they undergo changes.

Review client list: Print out a customer list with the services they have and determine other products that provide value. Identify and prioritize the top twenty opportunities. Each month, be proactive with your clients and approach those with potential for you to add business.

Build several relationships within clients: Meet with many people within an organization to better understand how your services can help achieve their corporate objectives.

Build relationships high, wide, and deep among your clients and recognize that your current contact may be promoted or leave.

Communicate with customers and keep them abreast of industry changes and especially of enhancements to your products. Treat them like a valued customer and they will be. Never take a client for granted.

Become their "trusted advisor." That is, one they can count on to provide them current information and advice on what is best for them, regardless whether it is your product or not. In the long run, you will be rewarded with more business.

"Approach each customer with the idea of helping him or her to solve a problem, not of selling a product or service."

Brian Tracy

Acres of Diamonds is a story of a man who sold his farm with a riverbed to seek treasure throughout the world. The person who bought his farm discovered gold in the stream. Look around at your current client situation to find acres of diamonds.

C. IDEAL CUSTOMER PROFILE (ICP)

Determine what characteristics you would like a customer to have. The profile of an ideal customer may include; location, size of company, income, need for product, average revenue per sale, solid profitability for the company, and a need for additional products and services.

The secret is to prospect to those who need your product or service, who can make a decision to purchase and have the ability to pay.

Rank prospects: You may use the A, B, C system, to qualify and rank prospects and customers. Your contact management program should enable you to sort and highlight those prospects for follow-up.

A. **Meets Qualifying Criteria**

B. **Meets Some but Not All Criteria**

C. **Does Not Meet Criteria**

The secret is to establish a coded system to qualify and quantify prospects and clients.

Able to pay: Does your prospect have a history of paying late and struggling financially? Check them out through credit agencies to determine their financial stability. Don't be guilty of a rookie mistake by selling to one who doesn't pay and have it haunt you.

D. DISCOVERY QUESTIONNAIRE

Identify the prospect's needs using a comprehensive discovery questionnaire. Until you fully understand the obstacles your prospect faces, it is nearly impossible to provide effective solutions.

List the main people who will impact the decision to buy: CEO, CFO, CMO, CIO, president, etc. Gather background information on the prospect to include the SIC code, current vendor, potential needs, etc..

Company Name   **Address**   **Contact**   **SIC Code**   **#EEs**

E. QUALIFY PROSPECTS AND CLIENTS

Qualify prospects over the phone within 3-5 minutes by asking a few relevant questions. Control your destiny by controlling your calls and the time you spend on them.

Question and Listen: After you provide your marketing message and the client understands what you do, it's time to determine if you can help them by asking questions.

Prepare key questions:

- What? What are your major challenges?

- Where? Is this a local or national issue?
- When? When did this happen?
- Why? Why is that a problem?
- How? How do you plan to change the process?
- Who? Who is in charge of that task?

Listening to answers is a trait that successful people share as they become more informed, better able to nurture relationships and achieve more.

Identify needs: Uncover the problems that face the prospect. Ask: "Under ideal circumstance, what would you like to see happen?"

As Doug Larsen said, *"Wisdom is the reward you get for a lifetime of listening when you'd preferred to talk."*

If the prospect does not meet your qualifications, move on to the next call.

F. DEVELOP SOLUTIONS

Your immediate goal is to solve the client's' problem through your product solution.

Provide solutions: Based on your discovery, it's time to provide solutions to match the expressed needs. Determine the most appropriate set of services to resolve their issues.

G. PREPARE PROPOSAL

Your proposal provides specific products to help prospects alleviate their problem and begin to achieve their goals. Ensure your proposal includes all the required information for a person to decide. For example: provide details of products and services, common questions and answers and an application to purchase your products or services.

H. SALES PRESENTATION

Presentations to a prospect, client, or distributor for a specific sale of a product or service are critical in the sales process. Chapter XI provides more details on making effective sales presentations.

Many salespeople make one-on-one presentations but the complexity of each sale may include people from various departments to provide input and answer questions.

For example, if you are selling a complex system, it would be helpful to have someone from your IT department to respond to more technical questions. An accounting person may be helpful when presenting financial programs. Include those who are more technical when presenting more complex products or services.

I. SALES FORECAST

To report your sales forecast, determine what is sold, promising or dead. These guidelines help to focus sales efforts on prospects likely to purchase. An alphabetical method or percentages to assign them an A, B, C or D to reflect their status.

A. Sold. Contract is signed and completed. 100%

B. Verbal Commitment. Contract is in process. 80%

C. Promising. Potential, but no formal commitment. 50%

D. Dead. Prospect does not meet criteria.

J. FOLLOW-UP

After you present your proposal, follow-up with the prospect to determine their level of interest within 24-72 hours later.

Don't Give Up: Be prepared to overcome several objections and continue to pursue the buyer. Studies show that 43% of sales people give up after the first sales call and 60% of buyers say NO before saying Yes.

If you are not awarded the business, ask them why and what you could have done better to gain their business. Their response may be enlightening and help you improve.

K. THANK YOU

After a new sale, send a handwritten thank-you note to the customer and each person who assisted in the sale. This is always appreciated.

Now that you have become a trusted advisor and lived up to or exceeded expectations, your credibility will be high and the client will think positively of your ability to deliver as promised.

IV. SALES STRATEGIES

"Nothing is particularly hard if you divide it into smaller jobs."
Henry Ford

A. DEVELOP PROFESSIONAL RELATIONSHIPS

Favorable relationships with prospects are often the critical difference when selecting a vendor. As more products become commodities, positive relationships become a deciding factor.

Know their hobbies and provide tickets to sporting events, concerts, and other activities.

- ✓ **Know family members.**
- ✓ **Know personal interests.**
- ✓ **Contact often.**

Build better relationships with email notices, monthly newsletters, sending birthday and Christmas cards and, most importantly, contact and visit them regularly. In some instances, your professional relationship will extend to a personal one as well.

B. DISTRIBUTION CHANNELS

Several factors should be considered when deciding how to approach the market.

Direct: Going direct to the prospect or customer is often the preferred method as a proprietary sales team can best describe their products and services and overcome objections.

This approach requires a commitment to train staff on the features and benefits of products and how to represent the company.

Brokers/Distributors: Brokers and manufacturers' reps can be profitable distribution channels to remarket products and services. They are typically paid a fee or commission. This approach lowers your direct cost of acquiring new business and gets into more accounts faster.

Seek out those brokers who control a lot of the business in your markets. Identify distributors in each city through industry journals and develop a strategy to meet them to develop a relationship.

Treat brokers and distributors just like other prospects. Discover their challenges, provide an overview of your products and services and describe your Ideal Customer.

Ask probing questions about the products the brokers or distributor represents. Identify their primary customers and ascertain what is required for your products to be their leading ones.

- **What is their target market?**
- **What do they want from a service provider?**
- **Are their recommendations based on price, commissions, and references, or other factors?**
- **Do they tend to favor one vendor all the time? Why?**

In short, align your products and services with those brokers and distributors who support yours and can generate sales. In some instances, their markets are broader than the ones you market to and that can expand the potential for greater sales.

C. TELEPHONE TECHNIQUES

If you use a cell phone to schedule tasks and activities, learn the many features that are available but are not fully utilized.

Use caller ID to screen calls. When involved in a project, don't take phone calls unless caller ID identifies someone you need or want to talk with. It takes more time to get back into a project when interrupted. Let the call go to voice mail and return calls as your schedule allows.

Avoid Telephone Tag: Telephone calls can be handled more efficiently by using voice mail more effectively. Many just leave a name and phone number to call.

When you make a call or respond to voice mail, leave a detailed message rather than just your name. Be specific on what you need so a person can begin to work on satisfying your request. Likewise, if a request is made for you to complete, prepare a detailed response.

Call in Bunches: Place and return phone calls in bunches at a specified time. It's an effective time saver and avoids interrupting projects. Just before lunch is ideal because people are in a hurry to eat and are less likely to chat. Return calls before the end of the day to be responsive plus it gives you peace of mind in the evening.

When making a call, get to the point and say, "I know you are busy, the purpose of my call is…"

To get off the phone say, "Let me let you go," or "I will talk with you later, etc."

Telephone Campaigns: These are an integral part of a successful salesperson's prospecting program. Many salespeople have "call reluctance," a fear of using the telephone to contact a prospect. Call reluctance can be overcome with a well-designed and rehearsed telephone presentation. You will soon be able to handle virtually any situation.

Write presentation: Write out your telephone presentation and practice it aloud to improve. If you simply call and 'wing it' you will not have success and future calls will be ignored.

The secret is to make perfectly rehearsed messages so each word motivates the prospect to talk with you.

Practice: Practice your sales statement or marketing message and make it consistent and compelling so it is clear how you help companies and individuals succeed.

Be prepared with information on your company such as how long you have been in business, the number of customers you serve and how others have benefitted from your services or products. Include testimonials that enhance your reputation.

Telephone Tips/Etiquette. Use the following techniques to improve making appointments, to qualify prospects and identify the key persons within an organization.

- ✓ **Provide Your Name and Company**
- ✓ **Request Time to Speak**
- ✓ **State Your Marketing Message**
- ✓ **Ask to Speak to The Appropriate Person**
- ✓ **Question and Qualify**

Provide Your Name and Company: State your name and your company name so they know who you are and the company you represent.

Ask to Speak to The Appropriate Person: Use your marketing message so the listener understands the purpose of the call and can refer you to the appropriate person.

Example: *"I am James Smith with ABC Company. Our company has developed a unique method to reduce health care costs to companies. Am I speaking to the appropriate person who has responsibility for these decisions?"*

Request Time to Speak: When connected to your desired contact, always ask if the person has time to speak. "May I have a moment of your time?" This is a courtesy that many others ignore.

State Your Marketing Message: Get to the point and provide your Marketing Message to include features and benefits of your products and/or services so the prospect clearly understands what you provide. Display confidence.

Question and Qualify: Your message should be planned, rehearsed, and presented in a convincing manner. Prepare questions to qualify a prospect. If the prospect qualifies, ask for an appointment to further discuss the prospect challenges and potential solutions to help resolve their problems. If the prospect does not meet your Ideal Customer criteria, move on.

D. DIRECT MAIL

A well-designed direct mail campaign targets several people within a prospect. Approach the buyers and the highest-ranking people in the organization such as the CEO, president, COO or CFO.

"High and Wide" Approach: High and wide best describes how to target key executives. Ensure that those who may be affected by your service know its potential.

The secret is to approach the highest-ranking people.

However, if you have a current relationship, don't go over their head unless you are not making any progress toward a sale.

Headline Benefits: Grab their attention with a headline or opening sentence that describes what a prospect will gain with your product or service. For example: save them money, reduce their staff, improve quality, lower their costs and/or increase the speed to process? The reader will be interested when you provide specific benefits to help their business.

- **Higher Sales**
- **Improve Revenue**
- **Reduce Costs**
- **Increase Productivity**

Overview: Letters can help qualify prospects when you provide an overview of your product line and offer an incentive for them to call you, to go to your web site or take your follow-up phone call.

Specific Solutions: When you provide a specific solution to a problem, the CEO may forward the letter to the appropriate person to determine if the benefits will help achieve their goals.

Compelling Benefits: If your message is compelling and your service or product will benefit prospects, they will want to know more. Occasionally, they will call you and ask for an appointment.

Congratulations: When you see an article about a person or his/her company, send it along with a personal note of congratulations on their achievement.

Track Campaigns: A mail campaign is a method to generate leads but determine the effectiveness of direct letter mail campaigns by tracking mailings and the number of sales.

Test Campaigns: Use different letters or special offers and "Test" each campaign and record the results prior to and then after the campaign and decide to expand or reduce a campaign.

Postcards: Mail companies can target prospects by location and income to focus your marketing efforts. Postcards are a good option for short messages, special sales or coming events such as a Grand Opening, etc.

E. SALES ACTIVITY

"You can't always control results but you can control activity."

Unknown

Monitor Sales Activity: Determine the level of sales activity required to generate sales. Sales activity can vary based on the sales position. For example, Telesales have a higher call frequency than those who travel and meet prospects face to face.

The critical sales activity measures are:

- **#Mailers/E-mail**
- **#Telephone Calls**
- **#Proposals**
- **#Face Calls**
- **#Presentations**
- **Close Ratio**

Track the results of your proposals and presentations and how many e-mails, mailers, telephone calls and face calls are required to close a sale. Ensure sales activity supports the goal of achieving sales, not simply making calls to satisfy activity measures. Maintain your focus on sales.

Call Activity: Record your call activity to determine how many phone calls you make to get a face call. How many proposals it takes to close a sale. Become more effective making good telephone calls and you can better maximize your time.

The secret is to track sales activity and results to assess where to spend your resources in sales campaigns.

Face Calls: Face-to-face calls with prospects are the most effective for closing sales, to build relationships, demonstrate products and establish credibility but are more difficult due to time constraints and expense, but they are key to outside sales.

Close Ratio: The close ratio is the percent of sales you make for each presentation, proposal or call you make. Be consistent in how you determine your close ratio. Improve your close ratio and you increase sales with the same level of sales activity.

Your close ratio is a function of your ability to qualify prospects, make effective presentations and close business.

Review Progress: Prepare reports to show sales results in terms of number of sales, average revenue per sale and close ratio, i.e., number of presentations to final sales. Compare your sales results and activities to that required by the company. Review reports to uncover shortcomings so you can take corrective action.

F. IMPLEMENTATION PLAN

Some sales are complex and require many actions to complete over time. Provide the new customer with an implementation plan and review the steps to be taken, the timeline for each activity and what is required by all parties to ensure a timely delivery of the product or service.

Determine a prospect's expectations to ensure they are in line with your ability to deliver. Contact the client at each step and update them on progress or delays through calls, email, text, etc.

Answer these questions and provide detail:

Who-Who will be involved in the transition team to implement the new service? This means from both the provider and the customer.

What-What service is provided? Explain the parameters of that service.

Where-Where will this process take place? Does it require resources from other departments, regions or corporate?

When-When will this occur? Provide a timeline and if the process is in graduated steps, ensure both parties know the expectations.

Why-Explain why the new service or product is important and restate the benefits to the company. This is helpful so others understand why they need to support this action.

How-How will the process work? What specific steps and due dates should be defined, so it is clear what each party must contribute to make this a successful implementation?

Give your customer peace of mind by providing a timeline for the implementation plan. Moreover, this plan will guide the implementation team as to the commitments made to the client. After you have completed a few plans, you will develop a template that requires only minor changes for subsequent clients.

The secret is to manage the implementation process and remain involved to ensure all parties meet their timelines.

SECTION B

MARKETING

V. MARKETING PLAN

"Coming together is a beginning; keeping together is progress; working together is success."

Henry Ford

A. OVERVIEW

The purpose of a marketing plan is to establish what is to be accomplished in the next one to three or more years. It assesses the market to determine its potential and updates the features and benefits of the products and services.

A market analysis defines the market potential to focus sales efforts. Competition is evaluated to determine how products and services compare and to list improvements to be competitive. Marketing materials are reviewed and completed professionally with a distinct look and functionality.

A training plan is established to ensure all persons are fully prepared to compete successfully. Finally, management reports are defined so a sales person and management fully understand the current status and be able to take corrective action when needed.

B. OBJECTIVES

Objectives may include sales goals, upgrading systems, improve implementation process, complete a sales training program and more. A plan may be several pages or a one-page document listing the key issues to complete. In short, be focused on what must be accomplished and the methods to achieve these objectives. An annual marketing plan should be reviewed quarterly to ensure all remain on track to achieve the objectives. Each year, the plan is reviewed and updated as needed.

C. PRODUCTS & SERVICES

List the products or services you sell in order of importance. Study each product or service to fully understand their features, benefits and pricing.

Features & Benefits: Assess the capabilities of your product and what it can do to resolve a client's problems. Distinguish between features and benefits. For example, a washing machine has a number of amps (feature) to save you time (feature or benefit) and reduces the cost to operate (benefit). The car tires have deeper tread (feature) to last longer (feature), to keep your family safe and save you money over time (benefit).

Expand Three Major Benefits. List three major features and benefits. For example: Save Money: low price, price match and free delivery. Now, add three more bullets to either support each of those key points or as additional ways to be competitive. **Add**: Increase productivity to reduce staff costs, money-back guarantee, free warranty protection, we will pick up old appliance for free, free hook-up. financing same as cash.

Bookend your key benefits. Present the three strongest benefits of your product with the most important benefit first, the third most important benefit second, and the second important point third. People remember the first and the last thing you say.

1. **Most Important Benefit**
2. **Third Most Important Benefit**
3. **Second Most Important Benefit**

D. UNIQUE SELLING PROPOSITION (USP)

Your USP for each product or service distinguishes what is unique about what you offer versus the competition. Describe the USP for each product or service. Most companies are strong in one particular area of expertise but not in all.

Identify a competitor's USP and position your presentation and marketing materials to diminish their advantage. Highlight your USP in your marketing message so prospects and clients remember how special your products and services are, e.g.:

- We offer the lowest price.
- Our products last longer than any competitor.
- Our service has the best guarantee.
- Our service is provided within 24 hours.
- Highest quality.
- Nationwide service.

The secret is to establish a USP, Unique Selling Proposition, for each product or service.

E. MARKET ANALYSIS

A market analysis enables you to focus your energy on those prospects that are most likely to purchase your products or services.

Gathering background information on prospects from a number of business sources will ensure that you screen out low potential suspects and focus on high return prospects.

Some of these sources include:

- **Internet**
- **Public Library**
- **Chamber of Commerce**
- **Department of Labor**
- **Dun & Bradstreet Listings**
- **USA Business Lists**
- **The Book of Lists-Business Chronicles**

1. Target Markets: To prospect effectively, first, define your target market. They may be steel manufacturers, software suppliers, or start-up companies.

Your target market may be a balance of small, medium and large prospects to include Fortune 500 companies, individuals, government agencies, professionals like doctors, lawyers, accountants, etc.

2. Market Segments: Determine market segments by number of employees, annual sales or location. Focus your energy on your top one-hundred prospects, customers, and distributors.

3. Target Audiences: Define your target audience by seeking out the person(s) in an organization who needs your service and can make a decision to buy. You may target all dentists, doctors, lawyers, HR managers, CEOs, CFOs, CIOs, as a target audience.

4. List Prospects: List each and why they are good prospects. Determine where the greatest number of opportunities are and devote more time and resources in those select markets.

Prepare a master list of suspects and begin to qualify them through research based on your Ideal Customer Profile.

a.   **List top 100 prospects**

b.   **Research to prioritize prospects**

c.   **Develop sales strategies**

Answer these questions in your market analysis:

1.   **What is your market share?**

2.   **Your market by size or industry?**

3.   **Where are your best prospects located?**

4.   **How many people live in each market?**

5.   **How many companies in each segment?**

6.   **What are the annual revenues?**

7.   **How many employees do they have?**

8.   **How many existing customers?**

9.   **Who are the key contacts?**

10. **Who are your competitors?**

Review the prospect's web site for names of the top officers to approach. Qualify prospects by A, B, or C and further by A-1, A-2, etc. Prepare sales strategies on how best to approach them.

F. COMPETITION:

Know your competition as well as your own company and compare them to your products or services. Their products may not have the same horsepower, size, capabilities or other features. Highlight those differences in a competitive situation.

Pricing: Compare your pricing model to your competitors. Some may use a bundled approach where their prices include many features or they may offer a base price with many features priced separately as add-ons.

You may think a competitor is higher or lower priced but a closer examination of the pricing model may result in being more competitive than the first look.

Explore the details of the pricing model to ensure you are comparing the same features and benefits so you can present your product or service in the most positive light.

G. MARKETING MATERIALS

Provide in your marketing materials features, benefits, USP and advantages your company offers.

Be Consistent.: Be consistent with your marketing materials. Use the same printer for all your needs; e.g., brochures, letterhead, proposals, business cards, etc.

Business Cards: Highlight (Bold) important information such as your name, phone number, email, website, and marketing message in larger font, at least 10 points. Avoid fonts and soft print that others can hardly read.

Prospect & Proposal Letters: Use the same font and type size, paper color, with same headings on each correspondence.

Virtual Assistant (VA): If these tasks are too daunting, consider using a VA as many of these tasks can be completed by or outsourced to a Virtual Assistant.

H. TRAINING NEEDS

Decide on the training needed to increase sales, e.g., improve prospecting, telephone techniques, etc. Assess jobs skills among the support team to ensure they are skilled at telephone skills, customer service, implementation process, and friendly to the customer.

I. MANAGEMENT REPORTS

Determine the information you need to measure results. You should review all pertinent information monthly but not less than quarterly. The full annual marketing plan should be reviewed quarterly to ensure everyone remains on track to achieve the objectives. These reports will include: number of sales, average revenue per sale, location of sale, size of company, type of industry, etc. Publish sales results for each sale rep versus their quota on a monthly and YTD basis.

Know your numbers. Set specific targets and measure them on a weekly, monthly, quarterly, and annual basis. Don't allow too much time to pass before reviewing the numbers. If you wait until the second quarter, you waited too long as there is little time to make changes to salvage the year.

I recommend a minimum of a quarterly review by senior management and at least monthly for a sales manager. I had a Friday meeting to review the progress on sales, especially the larger ones.

VI. MARKETING STRATEGIES

The secret to obtaining referrals, references and testimonials is to ASK for them.

A. REFERRALS

The number one secret for sales success is to obtain customer referrals.

Successful salespeople obtain referrals from satisfied clients to make more sales much faster. This also reduces the cold calling frequency. The confirmation of having performed successfully goes a long way in leveraging prospects into new customers.

Obtaining referrals is an inexpensive method to secure additional business. Ask your current clients, brokers, and suppliers to introduce you to others they know in the industry or community. Provide them with your business card and include your ideal customer criteria, e.g., "We serve small businesses in the IT field."

Positive comments from clients provide faster and deeper access so you can spend more time in front of qualified prospects. A simple request, "Can you think of 3-4 other people who could benefit from this service?"

One salesperson tied a red string to his briefcase to remind him to ask for referrals. Ask clients to provide an introduction by calling their friends and colleagues. Be sure to thank the person who provided you the referral and offer discounts or a special gift from your company.

B. REFERENCES

You will be asked for references; that is, people or companies who have used your product or service and are willing to support your claims.

In Requests for Proposals (RFPs), references are required. Have several quality ones readily available. Establish references by size of company, by industry, by service, etc. so you can tailor them based on the type of business you are pursuing.

References are an effective method to bolster your company's reputation but use them sparingly as these valued clients are only available for your best prospects.

Ask permission to use a client's positive remarks in promotional pieces or presentations. Provide their name, title, and company but exclude their phone number.

Publicize these comments throughout your marketing materials, newsletters, brochures, website, and podcasts. Sprinkle them throughout each page and use italics and bold type to reinforce each message. Include important comments to solidify your message and create credibility in the mind of the consumer.

> - **"Great Value"**
> - **"Best Investment"**
> - **"More than Expected."**
> - **"Had an Immediate Impact"**
> - **"Highly Recommended"**

C. TESTIMONIALS

Letters, emails, quotes, or survey results from customers are testimonials to support your superior services and products. Add them to your website, proposals, and presentations.

Customers often agree to provide testimonial letters but are uncertain how to prepare them. Provide a draft letter and suggest they add or delete whatever they think is appropriate. This technique simply provides a head start, yet the client feels the letter is their creation.

Testimonials can be gathered from your clients, distributors or company's customer service unit and replaces the need for prospects to contact references. An example of a testimonial may read:

Thank you very much for your product and your service. It was delivered on time and was set up by your staff so we were able to use it immediately.

We have already seen an improvement in our productivity and are realizing the savings you promised.

We highly recommend your product/service.

Sincerely,

Mary Smith, ABC Company

The secret to improve your results is to use your current customer list to obtain referrals, references and testimonials.

D. ADVERTISING

Advertising can be costly and a worthless exercise unless it is done carefully and professionally. "Test" market different promotions and determine which ones yield the greatest results. Profile the success of different ads to determine where and how to spend dollars. You will have a higher comfort level when your promotional dollars are spent wisely.

"Doing business without advertising is like winking at a girl in the dark. You know what you are doing, but nobody else does."

Stuart H. Britt

Use the Internet, business journals, newspapers, and other methods to advertise your business. Determine whether print, neighborhood mailers, flyers, post cards, newspapers, (neighbor, local and national) are cost effective by testing responses. Use Facebook, LinkedIn, Instagram to attract prospects by setting up your business page and POST frequently.

Use an advertising firm that specializes in your product and agrees with your campaign approach. Just as you are an expert in selling your products and service, ad firms are experts in their field of copywriting, graphic design, and ad placement. However, you must manage the process and be sure it fits your overall company strategy.

Track sales results for each ad campaign and assess which ads work best, where your best customers are located and what they purchased. Coding ads enable you to trace the origin of the promotion.

E. WEBSITE MARKETING

Use websites to build product awareness, to provide an overview of services and to market your products and services. Clearly define what you want your website to accomplish before you set it up.

Some will sell products directly while others gather contact information to send offerings. Your contact information may trigger a phone call to discuss the various products and services.

A small business owner must gain name recognition and that remains one of the most challenging obstacles to face.

Generate Traffic: Subscribe to services that provide key words or key phrases to trigger prospects to make contact.

Capture Contact Information: The website may be a lead generator to capture contact information to include name, address, phone number and email address. Then follow with updates and offerings of products and services.

Establish Credibility: Build credibility with testimonials on how your service solved a client's problem. Offer free advice and examples of success stories. Create an atmosphere of solution-based services by addressing the client problems.

Include ways the client can reduce their risk by offering money back guarantees, preview of your services for thirty days, free shipping and more.

FAQs: Include FAQs and answers to overcome common objections. These may number from ten to twenty or more.

Be Professional: Take the time, effort, and a little money to make an outstanding website. Use a professional to ensure the site functions as needed. A graphic designer can provide a professional appearance. Be sure it includes all the capabilities and ease of purchasing by linking to companies such as PayPal to take credit card payments.

Use Audio and Video to enhance the presentations. They enliven the website and guide the guest and highlights the key features, benefits and USP when comparing to competitors.

Provide Value: Offer discounts on your products and services when purchasing multiple products. Provide a menu of services but combine those that work best together. Include a time for taking advantage of a special offer to motivate them to make a purchase. Allow adequate time for a person or company to garner the funds. Sometimes it is a timing issue.

For example: Retired people receive a Social Security payment on a certain day of the month and they need time to receive their check.

Marketing Materials: Marketing materials on your website enhance your message and eliminates sending costly brochures to prospects.

The secret is to present your marketing message, phone number and website in bold and in large print on business cards.

Provide solution-based information on the needs and challenges of the customer.

Include background on your company to provide a comfort level that you are a legitimate business.

Make your marketing message compelling to satisfy the needs of your prospects.

Provide value by listing all the benefits and how it will solve a person's problems and make it easy for them to enjoy your product or service. If your price is higher, list the features that your product offers compared to your competitors.

Are your marketing materials consistent in appearance? For example, do your brochures, ads, letters, proposals, business cards, newsletters and website have the same look and feel?

Make it easy to do business with you and your company. Test your own website to ensure it delivers as promised by buying a product from it to see if it works.

F. PUBLICITY

Convey your message using press releases, articles for trade magazines, radio interviews, television appearances and as an expert reporters call regarding issues in your area of expertise.

Press Release: Use regional and local newspapers to announce the formation of your company, changes, and promotions.

Speakers Bureau: Enhance your reputation and become part of a speaker's bureau. Prepare a one-page overview of your product or service to highlight the most important. Add a summary of your background to establish your credibility.

Interviews: Provide Questions and Answers so the interview goes smoothly and is a great success.

G. NETWORKING

Networking can help gain new customers but it must be done with careful thought and consideration. When meeting others, ask questions about what challenges and problems they face and get to know them on a personal level as well.

> *"People do business with people they know and like.*
> *Get to know a lot of people and be likeable."*

Use your "elevator speech" the 15-30 second "value proposition" how your company provides solutions. Be more specific on what you provide "I help companies increase sales by 50% or more each year."

- **Know Purpose of Networking**
- **Ask About Their Business**
- **Use Your Marketing Message**
- **Qualify Prospects**

This exchange of information enables you to qualify prospects and follow-up with those who need your services. Get to know the key players in the networking arena as they are influential in the business community and will inform you of future events.

Look for organizations that include like-minded people who can be valuable prospects for your business. Chamber of Commerce, Rotary clubs, Kiwanis, and small business associations are all likely candidates for networking.

H. TRADE SHOWS AND SEMINARS

Trade shows and seminars can result in several leads. Assess the value of the show and determine what you want to accomplish, e.g., show your support for an industry organization, reach current customers, build brand awareness, research your competition, or develop new prospects.

Know your goals to determine whether to sponsor the event so your company name is prominently displayed.

Determine the materials to bring and your level of participation. Provide a drawing for a gift as this can garner business cards in a bowl for follow-up.

Companies use trade shows to showcase new products and enhancements. Use this time to pick up competitor's marketing materials and listen to their presentations. Gather ideas on how they are better than, worse than, or about the same as your products and services.

Provide this knowledge to the home office so they can assess it and consider product enhancements or pricing changes.

You may uncover one or two ideas that differentiate your products and enable you to share that with your sales force throughout the country.

Although many salespeople will only use some of the ideas contained in this chapter, it is important to be aware of the options available and used by others.

A strong marketing program will fit your company needs and helps meet overall objectives of the organization. Consider each carefully as they can be costly with little payback.

VII. PROSPECTING PRINCIPLES

"You can't build a reputation on what you are going to do."

Henry Ford

A. PROSPECT RESEARCH

You are expected to gather background information on the nature of a prospect prior to talking with them. Hoovers, Lexis-Nexis, Dun & Bradstreet and company websites are sources for background on a prospect's services, locations, financial data and more.

Completing research beforehand enables you to ask relevant questions that build credibility with a prospect. This step may eliminate prospects from your target list as not everyone will benefit from your services or meet your criteria.

B. PLAN TO PROSPECT

Top salespeople schedule time on their calendar to prospect each week and virtually nothing should get in its way. If another sales is pending, complete the transaction but prospect another time that week.

Mediocre salespeople generate a lot of activity and work those leads and stop prospecting. After closing a couple of sales, they must start their funnel from scratch and lose valuable time, production and income.

Conversely, the sales professional prospects continually to produce a steady list of qualified leads. Prospect to build a sales "funnel" or "pipeline" for a steady stream of sales.

"Keep your sales pipeline full by prospecting continually."
Brian Tracy

C. PRE-CALL PLAN

Develop a game plan before you make a sales call. Know the objective of each call, e.g., to move the prospect down the sales funnel from suspect to prospect and to customer status.

Define Product Scope: Make it crystal clear where your products and services excel so the prospect and/or broker knows your sweet spot. This avoids a lot of requests that you cannot fill.

Prepare Action Plans: Establish specific strategic plans and list action steps to achieve them. When goals and strategies are supported by specific action plans, you gain a higher comfort level for reaching them. These may include mailers to prospects, cold calls, contact current customers to add products, schedule presentations, etc.

D. BROKERS & DISTRIBUTORS

Apply the eighty-twenty (80/20) Pareto Principle and recognize that twenty percent of your brokers and distributors will provide eighty percent of your leads and sales. Don't treat all distributors the same. Spend eighty percent of your time marketing to the top twenty percent.

Compensation Plan: Understand how brokers and distributors get paid. Learn their commission scale and be certain that your company meets their expectations. Determine if competitors pay bonuses on top of commissions or you may be disqualified from being on their most favored list.

Like advertising, track results by each broker or distributor to ensure you maximize effort on those that yield the greatest return on your investment. Prioritizing them enables you to quickly identify those who provide the highest number of leads and sales.

E. VENDOR MANAGEMENT

The increasing number of vendors that companies work with is a major challenge. Strive to reduce that number with a total solution and you will gain more business.

- ✓ **Provide a spectrum of products.**
- ✓ **Offer lower cost & efficiency.**
- ✓ **Reduce the number of vendors.**
- ✓ **Eliminate competitors.**

An option is to ask prospects, customers, and distributors for thirty minutes of their time to present an overview of your entire product line. This positions you in a consultant role that provides the client alternatives to consider at that time or in the future.

An alternative is to approach them with a single solution you discovered that provides value to them or solves a problem.

If your presentation is proper, and your products are superior, clients will welcome the greater efficiency while reducing the number of vendors they deal with.

F. SAY NO TO BAD BUSINESS

Inform your prospects when your company does not provide the requested service or cannot meet their expectations. Some companies don't fit your ideal profile and never will.

Inform your brokers and distributors on what you can provide to save time from reviewing unwarranted proposals. Perhaps the prospect is too small, their credit rating is poor or they want custom products and yours are standard. Don't make a rookie mistake and promise more than you or your company can provide. Bring to the attention of management what the market requests and sell the products that are readily available.

Know what your company can and cannot do and represent that in your marketplace. The products you sell will meet the needs of most prospects. Don't fall into the "first year mistake" category and sell what you cannot support.

Once your brokers and distributors or customers know your sweet spot, they will do business with you because they can count on good service and a product that meets their needs. This is a win-win for everyone.

Be Prepared to Walk Away: Sometimes the best sale you make for the company is the one you walk away from. You cause internal operational difficulties when you sell the "one-off" solution that your company cannot service. Know when it doesn't make any sense to complete the deal under any terms.

VIII. TIME MANAGEMENT

*"What counts is not the number of hours you put in,
but how much you put in the hours."*

Theodore Roosevelt

A. OVERVIEW

You gain a sense of control over your professional and personal life by using effective time management techniques. Create a list of things to do; prioritize the tasks and complete the most important ones in the order of priority. This process will enable you to become more productive and enjoy peace of mind.

"It's more important to do the right things than to do things right."

Peter Drucker

Being more effective is doing the right things. Use your time to the fullest and complete those sales activities that yield the highest return; i.e., prospecting, planning, presentations, etc.

Being more efficient is doing things right. That is, when you complete a task, do it well. Examples include: a neat desk, a color-coded file system and other routine tasks.

"Getting ready is the secret of success."
Henry Ford

B. MASTER LIST

Develop a master list that includes all the tasks you must complete to achieve success. Write down each task and get it off your mind.

Your master list can be one long list of tasks or it can be sorted by topic that may include: proposals, prospecting, correspondence, filing, meetings, etc.

C. ASSESS VALUE OF TIME

Know the value of your time and understand the impact of using your time wisely. For example: to earn $100,000 a year, your time is worth $50 per hour.

- **2,000 working hours a year (50 weeks x 40 hours/week)**
- **$100,000 income=$50 per hour**

Work only on activities that yield $50 per hour. Filing, typing or other routine tasks can be done by someone making $15 per hour, or $30,000 per year.

Complete only the tasks that will help you meet your objectives that only you can do; that is, generate sales.

"Do not squander time, for that is the stuff life is made of."
Benjamin Franklin

D. GET ORGANIZED

To get organized, use planners, note pads, journals and/or a daily list of To Dos. Develop a planning process that covers your personal and business activities. Organizer companies that provide a full array of options include:

Franklin Covey	**Day Timer**	**Planner Pads**
At-A-Glance	**Day Runner**	**DATEBOOK**

For a salesperson who has several contacts that require taking good notes, Franklin-Covey is a comprehensive system whereas others are good for appointments and listing some activities.

E. PRIORITIZE WORK

Assess the importance of each task to ensure you remain focused on completing the most important and urgent tasks.

A-Priority: Important and Urgent

B-Priority: Important but Not Urgent

C-Priority: Urgent but Not Important

D-Priority: Not Urgent and Not Important

A-Priorities: **Important and Urgent**. Prioritize the list as an A-1, then A-2, and so forth. Work on the A-1 task until complete or you cannot work on it any further and then go to A-2, etc.

B-Priorities. Important but less urgent. There is no set deadline to meet; e.g., review competitor information, add FAQs or prepare objections with responses.

C-Priorities. Urgent but Not Important. Complete between A and B priorities such as filing, reading, etc.

D-Priorities. Not Urgent or Important. Eliminate these from work time; personal phone calls, web browsing, etc.

Think about your day and weeks and assess those tasks that must be completed. What your boss wants is usually a top priority. If you are the leader, you will be given many challenges to consider, and to consult with others and then prepare a plan for others to understand, and implement.

F. PLAN IN ADVANCE

Schedule your time weeks in advance rather than just the next day. Schedule presentations, meetings and activities two to four weeks or more in the future to increase your ability to meet your objectives. Poor performing reps wait until Monday to start working on the coming week. That is not for you.

Plan the Next Day: Before you leave each day, review your schedule, and gather last-minute items needed for the following day. Review proposals and presentations to ensure you are fully prepared. Update the PowerPoint, prepare copies of your presentation and gas up your car on the way home.

Save the last thirty minutes of each day to plan for the next day and complete the less important tasks such as filing, etc. This is how you "work smarter, not harder."

G. TERRITORY MANAGEMENT

Decide in advance the territory you cover and when you plan to visit. Identify the high priority customers, prospects and distributors and set appointments to maximize the use of your time.

Make good use of your travel time and meet many clients and prospects. Schedule several meetings: breakfast, coffee, lunch, afternoon, and dinner. Plan your travel in advance to get the best prices on airfares, rental cars, and hotels.

H. SCHEDULE TIME TO PLAN

Schedule time each day to plan your activities and write it down. Set aside time to prospect, review proposals, return phone calls or prepare for presentations.

The secret is to schedule in-house activities same as you schedule meetings, sales calls or presentations.

Initially, use Friday afternoons to review your territory, update customer and prospect lists, complete expense and activity reports, and read business literature. As you become more proficient, Friday afternoons are an excellent time to contact those hard-to-get prospects as they also spend that time planning activities.

Flexible Schedule: Build in time for unexpected events and emergencies. If your schedule is too tight, you won't have time to meet your obligations.

The secret is to schedule less than 60% of your time.

Schedule Office Time: Obtain a planner with fifteen (15) minute increments to complete more tasks. For example: review in-box, return phone calls, check emails, dictate a letter, review a proposal, etc.

- **Schedule tasks in the office to complete.**
- **Schedule in 15-minute increments.**
- **Manage your time in the office.**

I. PRIME TIME

Prime time, usually between nine a.m. and five p.m., is the best time for sales-related activities such as prospecting and making presentations.

Some executives are difficult to reach on the telephone as they have an effective "gatekeeper," a secretary or phone service. Senior executives and other leaders often arrive early in the morning and leave late in the evening. They may answer the phones before their support staff arrives and after their staff leaves for the day.

Non-prime time, such as early in the morning or later in the day, should be used to review proposals, develop special presentations, and follow up with others on needed information. List your tasks and prioritize them to determine the best time of day to complete them. Check your 'To Do' list regularly and select the most important 'A' task.

> *"We cannot do everything at once,*
> *but we can do something at once."*
> **Calvin Coolidge**

J. WORK LOG

An effective way to assess your activities is to keep a log of *everything* you do for a week or two. Typically, you'll discover that a large percentage of your time is spent on C-priorities. Refocus on A and B tasks and witness your productivity increase.

K. TECHNOLOGY

Technology such as laptops, cell phones, PowerPoint, video conferencing, e-mail, the Internet, and websites can improve your effectiveness. Seek training or hire an assistant to provide these services for you; website development, updates to FAQs, database tracking, sales support, answer calls, set appointments, arrange travel, etc.

Cell Phones: Cell phones are an excellent tool for phone numbers, information on clients, territory management, directions and sales reports. Capture and prioritize items. Learn the functionality of the instrument by going on-line for instructions and review the manual.

Internet Presentations: To make presentations via the Internet rather than in person is more commonplace. GoToMeetings.com offers this option. The future of sales will be via the Internet.

Sales Force Automation: Your sales force automation system can be invaluable in preparing customer lists and scheduling sales calls. Tools to plan, prospect and collect data, prepare mailing lists, sort prospects, and update your contact information should be fully utilized. Sales activity and expense reports are prepared in minutes when the information is entered regularly. Learn to use these tools to maximize your effectiveness and save time.

L. DELEGATION

Too often, people complete tasks themselves rather than enable others to complete them. Delegating tasks develops your staff to assume more responsibility. Delegate tasks early in the day for others to complete while you work on other projects. An assistant can prepare proposals, type letters and file materials while you are completing 'A' priority tasks such as talking with prospects and clients. Review progress during the day and make corrections to prepare final materials for distribution.

8-9 a.m. Prepare materials for others to complete.

1-2 p.m. Review materials and make changes.

4-5 p.m. Final review and distribution.

Define Tasks: To effectively delegate, ensure specific guidelines are provided. The experience of the staff member will determine how detailed the instructions. A good rule is to tell an experienced person what you want but not how to do it. For a less experienced person, provide more supervision initially.

Give your staff time to fail and to make corrections. Although it takes longer the first time to delegate work rather than do it yourself, the quality of the work will gradually improve. This frees up more time for you to work on higher priority items.

M. PAPERWORK

Try using the STAR method to handle paperwork.

- **S**uspense
- **T**rash
- **A**ction
- **R**eading

S-Suspense: Create a file for tasks to set aside when work is interrupted. This may include incomplete proposals, unresolved customer service issues or a proposal.

T-Trash: Throw away any unneeded papers. Don't put papers in a pile somewhere and think you will come back to them later.

A-Action: Include letters, contracts, or expense reports for your signature. Reply to routine paperwork by adding a handwritten note on the paper and direct it to others or return it to the sender.

R-Reading: Designate a file for material to read and schedule time to review the file. Tear articles from magazines and file them for review. Skim articles to capture the highlights. If you haven't touched the materials after a month, toss them or file for reference.

The secret is to review the SUSPENSE file daily to ensure that all outstanding work is completed.

N. FILE SYSTEMS

A proper filing system allows you to move paperwork from the in-basket to the out-basket and retrieve it when needed.

Put an "F" for File on each piece of paper to be filed and place it in a 'FILE' folder. Then pass it to your assistant or take ten minutes at the end of each day to file.

Effective methods for filing and retrieving information are:

1. Touch Paper Once: The best method is to handle the paper once and move it forward or to one of your files.

2. Use A Check Mark: Use the check mark method, whereby each time you touch the same piece of paper, you put a check mark on it. When you get tired of seeing check marks, you will do something with it.

3. Alphabetical Order: Set up a separate file for each client, prospect, or distributor in alphabetical order.

4. Subject Matter: File information by topic such as: federal regulations, state regulations, PowerPoint presentation, sales brochures, contracts, etc.

5. January-December and 1-31: Plan your year by using a monthly file and include notes each month to remind you of report deadlines, major activities, etc. Handle daily tasks by using file folders numbered 1-31 for a daily file system. Use to capture ideas, deadlines and tasks to complete using notes, or three-by-five cards.

The secret is to retrieve and review the FILE folder daily to remind you of tasks to be completed.

O. INTERRUPTIONS

Interruptions are big time wasters. Close the door to your office or if you work in a cubicle, put up a sign that politely but firmly states, "PLEASE DO NOT INTERRUPT-WORKING ON HIGH PRIORITIES."

Consider yourself an independent contractor who is successful based on how you use your time.

<u>The secret: Don't allow co-workers determine your success.</u>

Remain Standing: When people come to your office, stand up and talk with them through their first issue and then escort them to the door when finished. Meet later to discuss the issue in more detail. If you ask them to sit, it is hard to get rid of them.

Visit Other People: When you need information from someone, go to their office or workstation rather than request they come to your office. This allows you to leave when you choose.

IX. CUSTOMER SERVICE

"Two-thirds of companies stop using a service because they have a perception that the vendor does not value the customer relationship."

Michael LeBeouf, The Greatest Management Principle

A. OVERVIEW

The best companies consider customer service essential to their continued success. When customer service is poor, the company struggles to grow and when a new client is added, another one goes out the back door.

A new customer should be treated professionally to ensure they have a pleasant experience. Existing clients should be treasured and preserved as they are part of your growth strategy.

B. TELEPHONE SYSTEMS

Despite all the bad publicity about automated telephone systems, companies continue to make customers jump through hoops. Going through the vortex of a system is frustrating and more companies should make it easier to use the automated system or talk to a real person.

C. EASY TO DO BUSINESS WITH

One or two clicks of the mouse or someone answering the telephone should be all that is required to make a purchase or get assistance.

The CEO and executives should be required to use their system to order a product to experience how their system works or doesn't.

D. RESPOND QUICKLY

Respond promptly to customer calls and inform them that you received their message. Don't assume their deadline so ask when they need a response. Generally, when you receive requests via letter, telephone, or e-mail, respond in the same manner as the request. If it is a legal question, it must always be documented in writing after the legal department has reviewed it.

E. PROVIDE DETAILS

When a concern arises about your product or service the professional salesperson gathers the facts, prepares a comprehensive memo and requests a resolution. For example:

Sally Jones at ABC Company, client number 1234567, states that their February bill shows a double entry for item 3654. They received only one order but were charged for two. She requests we either credit her account for the extra charge or send another of the same item 3654 at no cost. She needs an answer by next Tuesday, since she must close her books for the month. Please send a response to her, with a copy to me. Thank you for your cooperation.

F. PLAN CUSTOMER CALLS

A simple chart allows you to plan customer calls. Enter a list of customers vertically and the month to contact them across the top of the page. After a call is completed, enter the date. Separate your customers into territories to better manage your visits. Schedule meetings with your customers to uncover or resolve problems or to add other products or services.

Be sure to bring pen and paper to take notes to ensure you capture all relevant information to resolve a problem. And always have order forms if the client requests additional products or services.

G. RESELL CALLS

Clients that must be resold each year require you to visit them at 2-3 months prior to the anniversary date. Prepare in detail why a rate adjustment is warranted.

H. SERVICE CALLS

Some sales professionals also service what they sell. In the eyes of the customer, the salesperson represents the company and they look to the person who sold them to fix any issues.

Others demand continued enhancements or regular service calls so the client remains happy and doesn't consider a competitor's offering.

Ask your customer service unit to alert you if a client has contacted them with a concern, especially if it has not been resolved.

I. CONTACT REGULARLY

Contact customers in accordance with their expectations. The most effective way to determine their needs is to ask how often they would like you to contact them.

Call your customers periodically and take them to lunch to assess progress or challenges and keep them abreast of changes within the company or industry. Retaining current customers is far less costly than selling new ones.

"There is no traffic jam on the extra mile."
Brian Tracy

J. COMPETITION

Determine if competitors have been talking with your clients. Gather information regarding your competitor's product improvements, pricing strategies or other enhancements and pass it along to your company to ensure you remain competitive.

SECTION C

PROFESSIONAL DEVELOPMENT

X. PRESENTATION TECHNIQUES

"Winston Churchill has spent a liftime
coming up with a spontaneous remark."
Unknown

A. OVERVIEW/A.I.D.A.

Make effective presentations and you will become more confident, more credible, and more professional.

Many people fear making presentations but when you know the content of your presentation in depth, you will present with confidence. One method to reach your audience is to use the A-I-D-A approach. A-Attention, I-Interest, D-Desire, A-Action.

Attention: Use your "elevator speech" the 15-30 second rehearsed message that describes your solutions for companies. For example, "We help companies reduce their health care costs."

Interest: Provide the best features and benefits and some examples how it benefited other companies. Ask questions to better understand what problems the prospect faces and determine whether you can solve them.

Desire: If your services can benefit them, explain *How* you can solve their problems. Provide testimonials where you improved another client's situation. Your presentation should be tailored to each specific company and their needs.

Action: Exchange business cards and contact information. Arrange for a follow-up meeting or schedule a presentation to recommend specific solutions and describe the action steps to be taken.

B. PERSONALITY TYPES

There are Type A's who are more dominant and Type B's who are lower key and others in between. Understanding the different personalities will improve your effectiveness.

CEO-Chief Executive Officer. Dominant, the decision maker, expects your service to improve the top and the bottom line and less concerned about how it will be completed.

CFO-Chief Financial Officer. Wants to know the cost, the impact on profit, how many resources it will take to implement, how long it will take. Be prepared with facts and figures.

COO-Chief Operating Officer/president. How will these changes impact the current operation, what departments are affected and who will do the work? Simplify the process and make it painless. Prepare an implementation plan.

CIO-Chief Information Officer. Concerned with how the new process will impact his backlog of projects. Bring someone from your IT staff to discuss the technical issues.

CMO-Chief Marketing Officer. They want what helps them sell more product and compete in the marketplace. Provide ways to improve efficiency with examples of success.

HR-Human Resources. They usually must get senior management approval and don't want to be shot down. Respect their needs and don't blow smoke. Be likable, engage in conversation and be thankful.

C. PRESENTATION TECHNIQUES

Understand the fundamentals of a good presentation to build self-confidence and impress your audience.

Overcome Fear: Although public speaking is the greatest fear of most people, there are many options available to improve these skills. Toastmasters, Dale Carnegie, Speakeasy, and other local public speaking seminars are resources to ensure you possess a professional approach.

A secret to overcoming fear is to mingle among the audience and introduce yourself prior to speaking.

Check Set-Up: Arrive early to ensure that the room is set up properly with equipment that is compatible with the power for your computer.

Power Position: Position yourself so your audience faces you so you can see their reaction as you speak. Take the appropriate place at the head of the table or in front of the room.

Smile: First, when you make a presentation, smile warmly to set a positive tone. Remember, people do business with people they like, so be friendly. If nervous, speak slowly to gain the breathing control needed for a professional speech.

Build Credibility: Build credibility by providing testimonials from other companies or individuals who successfully used your product or service.

Handouts: Don't provide handouts prior to the presentation as your audience will page through them while you talk and won't listen as intently. However, when technical information is provided or the audience is to take notes, provide materials in advance. An outline of the key issues and space to fill in the blanks keeps them engaged.

Become the expert and cite references, referrals, and case studies to enhance your credibility. Present examples of successful outcomes of your service.

- ✓ **Testimonials**
- ✓ **References**
- ✓ **Referrals**
- ✓ **Case Studies**
- ✓ **Guarantees**

Stand to Make Presentations: In David People's book, *Presentations Plus*, a study showed that when presenters stand and use visual aids, they are forty-three percent more effective in persuading the audience. Moreover, people are willing to pay twenty-six percent more money for the same product or service.

Avoid Distractions. Your speech should be authoritative while you take command of the meeting. Learn to stand still and do not pace or lean on a chair or put your hands in your pockets and jiggle your change. These distract and divert the listener's attention away from your message. You may move around but do so when you change topics or introduce another idea.

Posture: Maintain a solid and positive posture with feet shoulder width apart, weight evenly distributed on both feet and avoid moving your hands. Many people doing commercials on television keep their hands at their sides so they don't distract the viewer. It takes discipline, but it is worth it.

Dress for Success: Wear suitable attire to reflect that you are a professional and an expert. Carry a nice-looking briefcase or notepad, a good pen, comb your hair, shine your shoes, get rid of nose hairs and, when in doubt, overdress. You can always take off a jacket.

D. REHEARSE PRESENTATIONS

Rehearse at home in front of a mirror or with your spouse as your audience. Videotape yourself to see how well you present. Practice with your peers—your toughest audience—and allow them to ask questions. You will notice a significant improvement in a short time.

You will never be intimidated by an audience once you learn your presentation thoroughly. When interrupted with questions, you can handle them effectively and return to where you were without missing a beat.

The secret is to rehearse your comments and/or examples to support the value of your services.

E. THE PRESENTATION OPENING

State the purpose of the presentation, review the key points of a prior initial meeting and gain agreement on the issues. Provide any prior requested information at this time and respond to any questions.

Provide a comprehensive overview to include key benefits and advantages early in the presentation. A meeting may be cut short or questions take you in different directions and people leave the meeting, so be sure to cover the main issues up front and not wait until the end.

The secret to effective presentations is to know the first and the final two minutes to ensure a good start and a strong finish.

Just like the airline pilot whose biggest challenges are the take-off and landing, so is the opening and closing of your presentation.

F. POWERPOINT PRESENTATIONS

PowerPoint is helpful to provide background facts about your company; features and benefits of your products, key selling points, and why a prospect should buy from you. Customize it for each prospect when needed to make it meaningful and memorable.

PowerPoint is often used as a substitute for a compelling message rather than being a supportive role. Frequently, this canned approach is too long and lulls the audience into a state of anxiety.

If your audience and need to show your technology, PowerPoint can be effective for delivering your message and should be tailored to meet the prospects needs.

Limit Text: Secrets for making your PowerPoint more effective include using only 3-5 bullets per page and 5-7 words per bullet. Otherwise, each page is too busy and the audience will lose interest.

- **Limit Five Bullets Per Page**
- **Limit 5-7 Words Per Bullet**
- **Don't Read Bullets Verbatim**
- **Position Laptop to Read Screen**

Less professional presenters simply type sentences on their slides and read them verbatim by turning their back to the audience.

Use bullets instead, and illustrate each point with an example, story or anecdote.

Computer Screen Facing You: Avoid turning your back to the audience to read the bullets on the screen. Set your computer screen to face you so you can refer to it. Use a large display screen so audience members can easily view its contents. Ask the company in advance if they have equipment available to save you from lugging yours around.

G. EASELS

Easels can be highly effective to list key points, capture questions and write out key words and phrases. It is a lifesaver if your electronic equipment fails. Prepare your presentation in advance in case your computer fails.

Write out key ideas in pencil and flip to them when needed. As you speak, simply write over the pencil notes so you don't have to refer to your presentation. This appears more spontaneous.

✓ **Prepare presentation on an easel for backup.**

✓ **Write out key ideas in advance in pencil.**

✓ **Capture audience questions.**

Capture questions on the easel or in your notes to ensure you address the question and retrieve the information for your summary proposal.

Transcribe the key elements of the discussion points and add the questions to your library of FAQs. These vital bits of knowledge are used to prepare future presentations.

H. PROOF STATEMENTS

Be prepared to prove any of the statements you make. Cite specific articles or studies from which you obtained your facts. If you don't know the answer or cannot provide information, make a note of it and state that you will get back to them later either by e-mail or phone.

The secret is to have proof to support key points.

I. STORIES & TESTIMONIALS

As important as it is to know your products and be able to present them in a logical order, make them come alive with stories, experiences or examples of how your products benefited other customers.

A testimonial letter from a satisfied customer on how you saved them money, increased productivity or responded to their needs with timely customer service is invaluable. People remember examples of success, so provide real experiences to support each benefit of your product or service.

J. SUMMARIZE

Summarize the key points of your presentation and solutions that will satisfy the prospect objectives. Allow time for questions.

Ask open-ended questions to uncover objections. "What do you think?" Don't dismiss any questions. Many can say "Yes" but it just takes one to say "No." Restate the benefits to satisfy everyone's needs.

In the close, ask if there are any issues to address prior to moving forward. Be prepared with order forms, proposal, and a contract.

K. Example Presentation-See APPENDIX

XI. SALES PRESENTATION

"Few souls have been saved after the first twenty minutes of a sermon."

Mark Twain

A. OVERVIEW

The sales presentation is more specific and includes interaction with a reduced audience, often a one-on-one encounter. This requires as much or more preparation as the issues are tailored to a specific company or individual. Be prepared to provide comparisons of your product or service versus competitors.

When you need proprietary information, reassure them that their information is confidential and will not be shared. Bring a confidentiality agreement with you to assure them.

B. LENGTH OF SPEECHES

Determine the time you have for your presentation and allow 30-40% of time for questions whether at the end or during the presentation.

A 30 second introduction: Provide your name, company, Unique Selling Proposition (USP) and Marketing Message.

For example: "I'm Mary Smith with ABC Enterprises. We provide solutions for automating all aspects of the business process and can save clients millions of dollars."

The "**two-minute speech**" is a summary of the key benefits of your products and service. Offer examples and testimonials how you helped other organizations achieve success.

A "**five to 20-minute presentation**" summarizes the problems a prospect faces and includes specific solutions.

C. PLAN PRESENTATIONS

Consider your audience and provide what appeals to them that will compel the prospect to purchase your services. Prepare key advantages that differentiates you from your competition; save money, reduce staff, meet quality standards, improve service and pricing options.

D. KNOW YOUR INTRODUCTION

Thank the audience for the opportunity to meet with them. It is imperative that your opening is rehearsed to the point that you know it cold. Don't take a chance or "wing it," as it will show the prospect you have not prepared for them.

Make your introduction less than two minutes long and so compelling that if they heard nothing else they would want to buy your product. Include a welcome, an overview of what you are presenting and the structure of the presentation, e.g. will questions be allowed at any time or at the end of the talk.

Dale Carnegie courses teach how to make effective speeches in less than two minutes. Much can be said in that short period of time when you are prepared. However, this requires discipline and planning. Think how to summarize your life in two minutes; where born, when, hometown, sports, other activities, college, year and degree, jobs, hobbies, etc. You can do it but it would be more effective when planned and rehearsed.

E. PERSONAL INTRODUCTION

One technique to make a better connection with the audience is to make a more personal introduction. Provide your name, title and job responsibility, and add background information such as your hometown, hobbies, wife and kids, etc.

For example: *"Hello, I'm John Smith in charge of sales. I grew up in Naperville, Illinois, and graduated from Northwestern with a degree in business. My wife Sandra and I have two children. I have been with ABC Company for seven years, responsible for sales and marketing, and my hobbies include golf, hiking and tennis."*

You will find more common connections with your prospects in the first twenty minutes than you would over the next year. Try it.

F. MEET WITH THE DECISION MAKER

When scheduling the presentation, request that the person with the authority to buy is available. If not, reschedule the meeting. Remember, your time is valuable and cannot be wasted. You want to close the deal and relieve their pain so they can feel the gain.

G. KNOW YOUR PRODUCTS

Know your products thoroughly and be able to position the features and benefits to align with the client needs. It's critical to be able to present all products in detail. Being able to recite all the features are like feathers on a scale; they add up.

New reps make joint sales calls with sales managers and, as they listen, they think they can handle the presentation. But when in front of a prospect the words don't come as easily as expected.

Compare this to when you sing along with a song on the radio and can recite the words when the music is playing. But, if you turn down the volume, can you finish the song?

Only when you can complete the presentation on your own will you truly be in command of this phase of the sales process. You should be able to pick up on any feature or benefit of your products and compare them to the competition.

This takes practice and it becomes even easier if you write your own sales presentation. Practice and rehearse between appointments and emphasize those benefits that meet the client's needs. In short, know your products.

"If I miss one day's practice, I notice it.
If I miss two days, the critics notice it.
It I miss three days; the audience notices it."
Andrew Paderewski; Polish pianist-statesman.

H. OVERCOME OBJECTIONS

When you respond to a question, pause, restate the question to ensure that others heard it and then reply.

The secret is to be prepared to respond to questions from prospects.

The process to handle objections begins by listing the 10-20 or more most common objections and responses. Discuss these with your sales manager and other leading sales reps to get feedback and input on effective responses. Often, the hardest part is to develop positive responses but they make your sale more likely.

Capture new objections and prepare responses that place your product or service in a positive light. Soon you will have many Q&As and excellent responses for each product or service.

- **List common objections.**
- **Develop written responses.**
- **Add more objections and responses.**

As your products and services change, update the FAQs. You will gain the confidence to win more sales when able to overcome objections.

The secret is to resolve the buyer's issues so they are comfortable making a purchasing decision.

I. THE CLOSE

The final step in the presentation is the close. Consider your close before you begin to position the sales presentation.

Close-ended questions such as:

"What color did you have in mind?"

"When did you need to start or complete the installation?"

"Have you decided on which features you will need?"

"When do we start?"

"Where do we go from here?"

"What are the next steps in the approval process?"

This may result in a sale at that moment or uncover objections to address. Based on the questions, develop a sales strategy for your next meeting.

The Ben Franklin method of listing the pros and cons is still valid. These techniques are typically built into your proposal and presentation rather than at the end.

Review the financial portion of the deal and restate the benefits and then ask to authorize the agreement. Avoid using terms such as "contract" "signature" or any legalized term. Instead, use words such as "agreement," "authorize," etc.

Closing a deal is often the most feared part of the sale and some salespeople wait for the customer to suggest it. Rather, it is part of the sales process and must be met head-on and you will be glad you did.

Where needed, provide an implementation plan, and set expectations for the service. Give them a high comfort level that they made a good decision.

J. FOLLOW-UP ON LOST SALES

Determine why you lost a sale by calling the prospect and ask why they bought from someone else. Ask how you could have improved your offer or presentation and they will often tell you. Then it will be up to you to improve your skills and get the training you need to enhance your presentation capabilities.

When you follow up, inform the prospect that you are still interested if the vendor they selected does not live up to their promises.

Provide information that positions your company favorably in the event the competitor falters. Further, it provides a comfort level with the prospect that you will follow up in the future if you are awarded the business.

In summary, the most successful salespeople are those fully prepared when making presentations. It can move you from being one of the finalists to the company of choice.

"The first man gets the oyster; the second man gets the shell."

Andrew Carnegie

XII. NEGOTIATING TIPS

"The bitterness of poor quality remains long

after the sweetness of a cheap price is forgotten."

John Ruskin

A. OVERVIEW

The ability to negotiate successfully is important for closing profitable business. Average salespeople lead with their best price, assuming that the prospect may already have a low price and they don't want to lose the sale from the onset.

Prices may be spread-sheeted and you don't have much control over the bidding process. That is, prices are submitted and compared to competitors without much personal involvement from the salesperson.

Many government agencies and larger companies go through a bidding process. It is helpful if you know people involved with the bidding to get a "last look," i.e., an opportunity to gather additional information or change your pricing.

In many instances, haggling over terms and price is expected. Position yourself with your customers and prospects so you can negotiate the terms of your contract.

A competitor may submit an attractive low-price offer but often this does not include the same features, benefits, and other conditions as your product or service.

The secret is to establish what you want, understand the negotiating process and know the value of each feature of your products.

Remember, if you win business on price, you will lose business on price. Sell on value!

This is an example of how a customer can pay more for something and feel better than a person who paid less. You will see that it is important to know the value of each feature of your product and to present it favorably.

Assume you are selling a product for $2,000 and your prospect says, "I'll offer you $1,500 for that item." You respond, "Okay, I'll accept your offer." What happened? The person who bought the item felt he or she could have gotten it for less money by offering a lower amount and may even question the quality of the product.

You are concerned that you acted too quickly and afraid that your boss is going to accuse you of being an order taker and not a professional salesperson.

After you have learned all about your product, you approach the sale much differently. The next prospect says to you, "I'll offer you $1,500 for that $2,000 item." You respond, "Oh no, I couldn't let you have this item with its beautiful craftsmanship and quality for less than $1,900. It has a lifetime guarantee and we provide free installation."

The prospect proposes $1,800, and you agree on the price of $1,850. Now you and your boss are happy and the customer made a good deal. That is an effective negotiation.

B. WHY PROSPECTS BUY

Discover at least five reasons why a person or company is motivated to purchase your products or service. Be prepared to negotiate on each point, whether it is price, service, warranty, delivery time, systems support, or a host of other issues.

List why prospects have not purchased a product and what needs to change to overcome their objections. Inform management of these shortcomings so they undertake product enhancements. In some instances, you must study your products more closely and improve your presentation.

Many believe that price is the most important reason people buy but it is usually ranked about fifth when making a buying decision. Other reasons for making a purchase include:

1. **Reputation of vendor.**
2. **Quality of product.**
3. **Relationship between customer and company or staff.**
4. **Financial stability of company.**
5. **Price.**
6. **Warranties.**
7. **Customer service.**
8. **Guarantees.**

C. PREPARE NEGOTIATING POSITIONS

You must be in the ballpark with your pricing to begin the negotiating process. When price is a major consideration, strive to know where your pricing needs to be, to be competitive.

1. **The highest price that you would like to sell at.**
2. **The price you are willing to accept.**
3. **The walk-away price.**

D. KNOW VALUE OF PRODUCT FEATURES

Prepare to negotiate by learning the value of each feature and benefit of your products or services so you can negotiate each point. Compare the features being offered versus those of the competitors. Your pricing may include a three-year warranty while your competitor's warranty may be priced separately or for just one year.

E. ESTABLISH PRICING STRATEGIES

If people always bought products for the lowest price, we would all buy the cheapest car, the cheapest house, or the cheapest washing machine.

People want the best VALUE for their money.

When you know the value of your products, you can justify the price compared to the competition. Some features may be part of a package deal while others are sold separately.

Assess whether you will agree to adjust your price to compete with lower-priced brands. If your target market is at the high end of quality, features and price, then you may not be able to compete on price alone.

Beware of competitors using predatory pricing to enter a market to build market share or to simply add revenue and experience top line growth. They may be using a last-ditch effort to build up their revenues before being purchased or they may have simply decided on a new pricing strategy.

Some requested features cannot be provided at any cost as the special handling creates higher costs than the value of the service. In these instances, refer the prospect to another vendor.

F. NEGOTIATING TACTICS

1. Line Item Negotiating.

2. Negotiate In Small Increments.

3. Omit Weak Arguments.

4. Beware of Delay Tactics.

5. Higher Authority.

1. Line-Item Negotiating: Discover what the other person wants in total. Whenever possible, avoid negotiating by line item. This is best accomplished by saying "I understand your position on that, but let's come back to it later."

To move the process forward concede on less-costly items but always get something in return. Reserve the more expensive items to trade on price or to satisfy the major need of the prospect. You may agree to reduce the price on one if they purchase a second one at the same time. **The secret is to give up only one percent at a time, not ten percent.**

2. Negotiate in Small Increments: Too many salespeople give away too much too early, thinking that the buyer will jump at the chance to close the deal. In fact, the buyer thinks that if it was that easy to get a discount, they wonder how much more you will give up.

Ask for concessions for each percentage you give. "We can lower that price, if you agree to a three-year contract."

3. Omit Weak Arguments: Never present a weak argument as part of your negotiation. If you have three strong negotiating strengths, then use only those three points. Don't add others as they will distract the negotiations and the focus will be on the weak argument.

4. Beware of Delay Tactics: Know that your adversaries will delay decisions until late in the process to see how motivated you are to settle the deal. Foreign companies are especially adept at delaying a final deal until you are scheduled to leave. They think you don't want to depart empty handed.

The secret is: Don't set a definite time for settling all the issues.

If you are prepared to walk away then you can set a firm deadline. If you have the leverage, enter final discussions only when the other party agrees to terms.

5. Higher Authority: Effective negotiating tactics include the use of "higher authority" or "time out" strategies to step back to assess all the options. A "time out" allows you and your team time to regroup and reconsider all the variables in a less pressured environment. Call for a time out to "call your boss," a higher authority, even if you have the authority to make the deal. This move may help speed up the buying and selling process. Know that most of the agreement will come late in the process so don't get frustrated with lack of progress.

The secret is to know that 80% of the agreement will come in the final 20% of the negotiating period.

G. WIN-WIN

The most successful negotiations result when you achieve a win-win outcome with a satisfied customer and your company prospers. Good clients understand and appreciate that you are giving them favorable terms while still supporting your company values.

You must be prepared to play hard ball with some vendors and be more conciliatory with others. It is critical to get the decision-maker involved to discuss your offering.

Don't take customers for granted. That is, don't assume that they will stay with you forever especially if you give lower pricing to new customers and raise prices on clients. They will test the market and if they sense you are unfair to them, they will leave and never come back.

Treat each customer just like a new one. Always provide your best service, keep prices fair and you will be rewarded with a long-term customer.

A happy customer purchased something;

An unhappy customer was sold something.

XIII. COMMUNICATION SKILLS

*"Let your discourse with men of business
be short and comprehensive."*

George Washington

A. OVERVIEW

Effective communication can be the most important aspect of your career. How well you convey your message can determine the level of success you achieve.

Writing letters to prospects and customers to grab and keep their attention, interacting with brokers and distributors and to communicate within your own company requires strong communication skills.

> ➤ **Prospects and Customers.**

> ➤ **Brokers and Distributors.**

> ➤ **Employees, Peers, and Superiors.**

Completing your resume without spelling, grammatical or punctuation errors creates a favorable impression and may land you a job.

Some companies now require you write an overview of your background before you are hired to determine your writing capabilities. They assume that if you cannot write properly when you apply for a position, you are unlikely to perform well on the job. Without these skills, you will be passed over for major projects and limit your career.

Become an effective communicator in writing, personal interaction and listening and do them all well. Make the commitment that your correspondence will be thorough and professional. Remember that only *you* are responsible for the content of the written communication.

How to Write Attention-Getting Memos, Letters and Emails

by

Arthur H. Bell, PH.D. is an excellent reference guide.

B. COMMUNICATION GUIDELINES

These recommendations apply to virtually all communication methods to include emails, memorandums, and letters to employees, customers and prospects. Review these principles when you prepare correspondence until you have them firmly in your mind.

1. **WIIFM**
2. **Plan Correspondence**
3. **Assume Wide Distribution**
4. **Omit Inflammatory Comments**
5. **Avoid Misspelling**
6. **Proofread**

1. **WIIFM:** Your reader is asking "WIIIFM." What Is In It For Me? Address that question in the first paragraph and your correspondence will be read. Express clearly why a prospect should read more than the first paragraph. Will you save them money, reduce their staffing costs or provide other solutions to their problems?

2. **Plan Correspondence**: Determine the most favorable format to develop or respond to a letter, report, email, or cover memo.

Typically, respond in the same manner the correspondence was sent to you. If you received a letter, respond by letter, if by email, respond by email, etc.

Upon receipt, inform the sender that you received their letter, call, email, etc. Even if you don't have an immediate answer, let the person know that you are acting on the issue.

The professional prepares ideas thoroughly, presents them in order of priority and recommends a solution. Be sure to give careful thought to how your message will be perceived. Too many people use poor sentence structure, include several ideas per paragraph, overlook typos in an almost incoherent message. Those who receive disjointed correspondence resent it and assume you don't care enough to prepare a professional response.

3. Assume Wide Distribution: Your correspondence may be sent to others in the company including your boss and the CEO. With the increase in the number of e-mails, send them only to the people who need to know. Don't send a blind copy to others unless requested to do so by your manager.

4. Avoid Inflammatory Comments: Your communication must be free of any inflammatory comments. Be respectful and less abrasive and omit editorial comments so your intended message is clear. Simply state the facts and request an action and others will be more willing to help.

When upset, prepare your thoughts on paper, and set it aside. Reread it later and replace negative words with positive and factual information. Pretend you are sending it to your best friend and your tone will soften.

"Never answer a letter (email) while you are angry."
Chinese proverb

5. Avoid Misspelling: Avoid misspelling words by using spell check, grammar check and by rereading your correspondence prior to sending. Spelling errors are inappropriate even for e-mail or memos.

Errors reflect poorly on the sender. Although email and memos are the most popular means to interact, the same guidelines used for more formal correspondence should be followed.

Commonly misspelled words:

- **Lose vs. Loose. You lose something, but something is loose.**
- **Role vs. Roll. Your role in the company. You roll the ball.**
- **Compliment vs. Complement. You can receive a compliment. Your product can complement others.**
- **Their vs. There. Their is person-related. There is a location.**
- **i.e. means, that is.**
- **e.g. means, for example.**

6. Proofread: Whether it is an annual business plan, a brochure, business card, email, letter or any piece of written material that reflects on you or your company, it must be reviewed for errors.

<u>**The secret is to always proofread your writing before you send it.**</u>

C. E-MAIL

E-mail is the method used to communicate virtually all messages to include the company strategy, Human Resource policies and everyday communication. However, e-mail is also becoming a stranglehold on the ability to get things done. Too many are sent to too many people.

1. **Review E-mails**
2. **One Issue Per Email**
3. **Combine Other Emails**

1. Review E-mails: Less thought is given to composing e-mails versus letters or memorandums. E-mails typically include typos, poorly worded sentences and readers are asked to review other attached emails to understand the topic. Review emails to ensure they are complete and free of errors prior to sending.

Jot down the intent of the email and put the emphasis at the beginning. E-mails should be short and to the point yet provide ample information so the reader understands the issue.

2. One Issue Per E-Mail: Type separate e-mails by subject so it can be stored in a file and easily retrieved.

3. Combine Other Emails. Combine a string of e-mails so the next reader can easily review the content. Your action will be appreciated and expect to receive a timelier response.

D. LETTER WRITING

Perhaps the most overlooked trait is the ability to craft a concise and effective letter. Too many salespeople cannot translate their product offerings and benefits to the written word. The fewer words used is always the most effective.

Each paragraph should begin with a topic sentence that is a mini heading for what you do and what benefit a customer will receive by using your service or product. Here are some important tips for improving your letter writing skills.

1. **Headline Grabs Attention**
2. **Call to Action**
3. **Bad News Letters**

1. **Headline Grabs Attention:** State the purpose of a letter early, even to the point of starting the letter with a headline. Just like a good headline in the newspaper can tell you the focus of the article, so does the opening in a letter. Try writing the main point of your letter in eight words or less. For example:

"INCREASE SALES BY 50% AND REDUCE COSTS."

Executives are too busy to read through paragraphs to get to your key idea. They want to know up front why they should continue reading. Save the history of your company and how many customers you serve for later. Use positive words such as:

Guarantee	**Proven**	**Reduce**	**Save**
Increase	**Quality**	**Advantage**	**Value**

I'm John Smith and I help companies save money on their employee benefits through auditing large health care claims.

Our unique selling advantage is that we don't get paid unless you save money. There are no upfront fees and we are reimbursed after you realize savings on your costs.

I welcome the opportunity to meet with you to further discuss how we can help your company increase profits by reducing your expenses.

I will be calling you within a few days to set up a time to discuss how we can save you money without any out of pocket costs to your company. I can be reached at (phone number and email address).

Sincerely,

2. Call to Action: Be sure you include a "call to action." At the end of the letter, ask them to make a call, look up your website or expect a call. This creates an expectation and moves the sales process forward.

Review your letters and ask others if your letters are professional. If you were the reader, would you continue to read the letter? If it doesn't grab *you*, rewrite your letter.

3. Bad News Letters: When a letter contains bad news, soften the blow by placing the bad news in the middle of the letter surrounded by other information that assures the reader that you carefully considered the issue and you ran it by your corporate legal staff, etc.

State that you evaluated the issue and cannot provide a full refund, but you are willing to give a discount on their next purchase. This is preferable to simply saying you can't help.

E. MEMORANDUMS

The memo format is distinct and the writing is concise. Clearly communicate your message and it will result in faster and more complete responses.

<u>The secret is to provide the purpose of the correspondence in the first sentence</u>.

<u>Date</u>:

<u>Memo for</u>: Name of person directed to

<u>Subject</u>: Title of subject, e.g., Recommendation for promotion, Complaint from ABC Company, Request for price concession, etc.

<u>From</u>: The name of person writing the memo

➢ **Include Purpose in First Paragraph:** Alert the reader what the issue is so they remain interested through the rest of the memo.

➢ **One Idea Per Paragraph:** Include only one idea per paragraph. Jot down all the ideas you wish to convey, organize them in order of importance and then write the memo.

➢ **Provide Detailed Information:** When information is incomplete, the reader will not fully understand what is requested and you'll receive an unsatisfactory answer. Provide details to support your key points.

Info to the home office. Use a memo to send information to the home office, especially when the prospect's needs are different from the standard product offering. Without specific information, the home office or manager cannot properly evaluate the issue.

Provide the needed facts and add your perspective of what the prospect wants and what specific issues will motivate them to buy.

Answer the following questions to ensure that the content contains enough information for someone to fully understand your message.

- ➢ **Who?**
- ➢ **What?**
- ➢ **Where?**
- ➢ **When?**
- ➢ **Why?**
- ➢ **How?**

F. MANAGER COMMUNICATION

Salespersons should respond to requests from sales managers quickly. These requests include; complete activity and sales reports, provide sales forecast, prepare expense vouchers, assess market trends, update competitor information and other requested items.

Often, your sales manager requests information because his boss is requesting it from him. As Zig Ziglar, a prominent sales trainer and author of many books on sales said, "The way to get what you want is to help others get what they want."

Managers may provide feedback and suggestions on how to improve. Pay attention as failure to act on the manager's ideas could result in not meeting your goals.

G. COMMUNICATE PROBLEMS

Your ability to communicate to management how the company can better serve clients may include:

1. **Customer service.**

2. **Competitor's features and benefits.**

3. **Are product prices competitive?**

4. **Do systems provide efficiency?**

5. **Are marketing campaigns effective?**

Your role of being the 'eyes and ears' of the customer is pivotal in presenting a reasoned approach for relaying client comments and suggestions to senior management. Inform management of issues regarding customer satisfaction, features and benefits, pricing, systems efficiency, marketing campaigns, etc.

When needed, provide specific examples of incidents; e.g. company name, date of incidents, products involved, attempts at resolution and recommendations for alleviating the problem.

Do not accuse anyone or any department of not doing their job. Simply state the issues and let the managers do their job.

Remember, the easiest department to run is somebody else's.

Problem-Solving: The PAR technique works when corresponding with someone to summarize the issue and action to take to resolve it.

- **P is for stating the Problem, concisely.**
- **A is for the Action that should occur.**
- **R is the Result or Resolution you desire or achieved.**

APPENDIX

APPENDIX A

SUMMARY

Although the information provided throughout the book covers many facets of the sales process and may appear to be overwhelming, it is critical that each chapter becomes part of your sales process.

It may take several months to fully grasp and master each phase as part of your pathway to success.

The first step of setting your goals and writing them down is critical to maintain your focus. Determining your target market and how to approach each prospect creates a process for initiating a sale.

A comprehensive marketing plan establishes a clear pathway for achieving success. It helps focus your effort on the type of prospect that makes an Ideal Customer and remain focused on those who provide the greatest return.

Learning the features and benefits of your products and services and being able to compare them to your competition enables you to make effective presentations and overcome any objections.

You can achieve your goals, meet all your obligations to your clients and your company yet still have plenty of time for family and friends by using proven time management principles.
The ability to make professional presentations takes effort but when you learn your products and those of your competition you gain the confidence to effectively compete.

Understanding the negotiating process ensures that your company prospers while still gaining the business.

Effectively communicating with the prospect, client and your administrative staff ensures your product is delivered and serviced as promised.

Learning the sales process provides you peace of mind, knowing that you can overcome virtually any obstacle you will face. I encourage you to begin the journey now and continue to implement the Critical Success Factors in this book and make them a part of your daily work life.

Embrace these concepts and you will enjoy higher sales, greater success, more advancement and provide a comfortable lifestyle for you and your family.

I truly hope you adopt these best practices and achieve the success you desire. There are no shortcuts in life and adopting these methods will make it easier to experience a life full of rewards beyond your wildest dreams.

In closing, when I was starting my sales career, I wish I had the information in this book. Now, you can develop a proven process for reaching your goals and advancing your career.

I wish you great success and a happy life.

Mark W. Shaughnessy

APPENDIX B

REFERENCE MATERIALS

BOOKS:

1. *The Time Trap*: Alec Mackenzie
2. *Secrets of Power Negotiating for Salespeople*:
    Roger Dawson
3. *How to Write Attention- Getting Memo's, Letters and E-mails*:
    Arthur H. Bell, Ph.D.
4. The Ultimate Sales Machine: Chet Holmes
5. *The Power to Get In*: Michael A. Boylan
6. *Presentations Plus*:-David A. Peoples
7. *The Sales Bible*: Jeffrey H. Gitomer
8. *The Client Nation*: Rico Pena
9. *Cold Calling is a Waste of Time*: Frank Rumbauskas
    www.nevercoldcallagain.com

TIME MANAGEMENT SYSTEMS:

a. Franklin Covey.com
b. Day Timers.com
c. Planner Pads.com

PUBLIC SPEAKING: Toastmasters, Dale Carnegie, Speakeasy

APPENDIX C

SALES SECRETS SUMMARY

Chapter I: Success Habits - 4

1. The secret is to continually learn new techniques. 5
2. The Secret to become a complete Sales Professional is to embrace all Critical Success Factors. 6
3. The secret to make a Quantum Leap is to discover new ways to market your products and services to qualified buyers. 8
4. The Secret is to focus your efforts on your top 20% of prospects and clients. 8
5. The Secret to Brainstorming is to allow ideas to flow freely and not to judge them as they are presented. 10
6. The secret is that some sales people are best suited for inside sales and others are outside sales oriented. 10
7. The Secret is to complete one task at a time to become more effective and efficient. 13

Chapter II: Goal Achievement - 15

8. Successful sales people clearly define their goals and develop specific strategies to accomplish them. 16
9. The Secret is to break down your goals into smaller amounts, write down your goals and strategies and review them daily. 18

Chapter III: Sales Process - 21

10. The Secret to sales is to quickly qualify a prospect, uncover a need and provide a solution to their problem quickly. 22
11. The secret is to prospect to those who need your product or service, can decide to purchase, and have the ability to pay. 25
12. The secret is to establish a coded system to qualify and quantify prospects and clients. 25

APPENDIX D

INDEX

APPENDIX E:

EXAMPLE PRESENTATION

Good morning, I am Mark Shaughnessy. I grew up in northeast Ohio and am a graduate of Kent State University. I'm a Vietnam veteran and have been married to my wife Lisa for about 40 years and we have two grown daughters. I live near Atlanta.

I am here to present how using Sales Secrets Today will enable your salespeople to increase their sales by 50% or more each year.

These methods are a result of being head of sales for Prudential and SVP of sales and marketing for Blue Cross & Blue Shield of Georgia, Jefferson-Pilot and Ceridian.

These fundamentals of sales were compiled to show that selling is a true profession and requires considerable effort, just as other professions do. Sales Secrets Today can be tailored to your specific company and the contents produced for your products and services.

The book can be distributed to all your employees so they are aware of the product features and benefits. This would include customer service, marketing and all managers, so everyone is on the same page. A Sales Secrets Today Workbook has been created that provide charts and graphs that can capture your best practices along with your product features, benefits and unique selling proposition that distinguishes your company from your competitors.

The summary page provides the cost and terms of the agreement that stipulates that if the process I provide does not meet your expectations, then a full refund will be honored. I simply ask that the entire program be implemented and I have an opportunity to assess the steps taken to ensure your salespeople have received the full program and embraced the concepts with commitment to the process.

Are there questions that I can answer?

"Would you like me to step out of the room while you consider this proposal?"